EASY RAMBLES

AROUND
WASDALE

MARY WELSH

QUESTA

ISBN 978-1-898808-30-5

Maps:
The maps accompanying the walks in this book are purely diagrammatic. Those for Walks 1-3 are reproduced by permission of Ordnance Survey on behalf of HMSO. © Crown copyright, 2009. All rights reserved. Ordnance Survey Licence number 100043743. The maps for Walks 4-10 are based on maps produced by Harvey Maps (Licence No. 80788/2 © Harvey Map Services Ltd., 2009)

Published by
Questa Publishing Limited
27 Camwood, Bamber Bridge,
Lancashire PR5 8LA

and printed by
Carnmor Print, 95/97 London Road, Preston,
Lancashire PR1 4BA

CONTENTS

NOTE

No attempt has been made to grade the walks in this book, as this is too subjective. Use the information about distance and height gain to calculate how long the walk will take. But also note, that these walks in Wasdale are more demanding than other walks in this 'Easy Rambles' series.

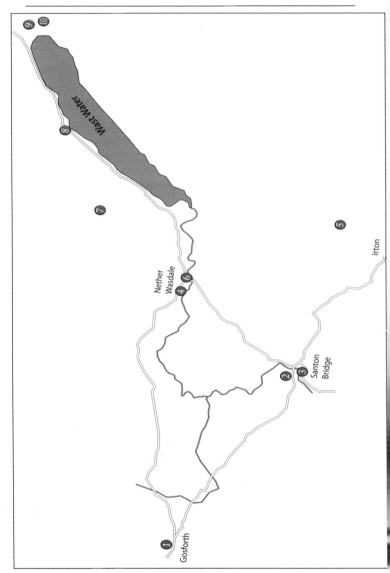

INTRODUCTION

Wasdale, once less well known to visitors to the Lake District, suddenly became very familiar to many television viewers when ITV ran a series of programmes on Great Britain's beauty spots, including Wast Water. The presenters asked viewers to vote for their favourite view. The overwhelming first choice was Wast Water and its wonderful semicircle of superb mountains overshadowing the head of the lake. The winning view was photographed from the foot of the Wast Water, taking in the lake and the mountains, making a charming picture, an unforgettable one. To enjoy the view that enchanted the nation attempt Walk 6.

As you continue along the fell road, with the lake lapping beside you, you feel the haunting presence of the Wast Water Screes, a 'wall', 600m high, of scree and huge awesome up-thrusting crags, all often splendidly reflected in the water on the opposite side of the lake. At first glance the Screes appear perpendicular, they are not completely vertical, but they are steep, and their slope continues for about 88m to the bed of the lake.

On your progress beside the lake, a road leads off towards Gosforth and just a short way along is the start of the walk to Middle Fell. This is a challenging walk, best done in good weather, and one that is wild and dramatic all the way. But it is also one that you can turn back if you find it too hard, having enjoyed what you have accomplished.

Just over half way along the lake, to your left, two fine becks hurtle down the fells to join Wast Water. These are Nether Beck and Over Beck, both full of cascades, waterfalls and rapids. They make for great walks but you need to stride their banks, up into the fells, to seek out their glory.

At the head of lake you feel the tremendous presence of the Scafells, Lingmell, Great Gable, Kirk Fell and Yewbarrow and perhaps this little book will tempt you to carrying on walking and to attempt to climb one or all of these tops in future.

As you walk beside the lake notice the change in the rocks and the vegetation. The high fells mentioned above and Illgill Head and its Screes, belong to the Borrowdale Volcanics. The slopes around the lake foot and beyond, are mainly Eskdale Granite. Look for the different material used for the stone walls at the head of the lake and compare it with the walls around Nether Wasdale. Both types of rock yielded differently to the pressures of the Ice Age glaciers, the latter responsible for gouging out Wast Water, this deepest of lakes.

Out of the lake flows the River Irt passing beside the village of Nether Wasdale, a scattered hamlet with a barn-shaped church, a maypole and two inns serving good food. The river continues through pleasing countryside explored by several walks in this book. It is joined near Hollins Bridge by the River Bleng, which rises north of Seatallan and Middlefell. The Bleng comes close to the thriving village of Gosforth, with its famous Viking Cross and Hogback Tombs.

The River Irt, swelled with the water of the Bleng, hurries beside Santon Bridge Inn from where two walks set off. One visits the remote 19th-century Irton church where in the graveyard stands a superb 9th-century Anglian cross. The second keeps close to the lovely river and strolls the countryside through which it dances. The Irt carries on to Holmrook and then makes a wide curve to join the sea at Ravenglass.

Scafell Pike is England's highest mountain, Wast Water the deepest lake. Two other facts where Wasdale achieves a first is the church at Wasdale Head (Walk 10) considered the smallest in Cumbria. The second is that here at the head of the lake lived the biggest liar in England. His name, Will Ritson. He once ran Wasdale Head Hotel and the spectacular waterfall beyond the hostelry is named after him. The annual Biggest Liar competition is now held at Santon Bridge Inn.

Wasdale is a challenging valley to walk compared with most other

Lakeland dales; here, the 'easiness' of these 'Easy Rambles' is a mite more demanding than elsewhere. Nevertheless, Wasdale has a haunting beauty, grandeur and quietness, which many walkers will greatly appreciate. It is more remote, and this should be remembered when setting off on walks.

The Right to Roam introduced to England and Wales between 2000 and 2005 has given access to many parts of the countryside that were once barred to walkers. This is true for the Lake District, and how much it has been appreciated by outdoor activists, be it canoeists, climbers or walkers. But with this right comes responsibility. We are reminded not to climb walls, break fences, stray into the curtilage of people's homes or drop litter. We are also asked to shut gates, walk in single file through hayfields and to leave nesting sites alone. Many of us like to walk the fells with our dogs and we are requested not to give our pets too much freedom but to keep them close to heel as we near a farm, horses, sheep, and cows particularly those suckling calves.

The walks in this book vary between 3½ miles and 6½ miles. The first walk in this book starts from the north-west of Wasdale and the following ones move steadily towards the mountainous head of the valley, though none attempt any really serious climbing. Below are the author's 'Golden Rules' for good safe walking:

Wear suitable clothes and take adequate waterproofs.
Walk in strong footwear; walking boots advisable.
Carry the relevant map.
Carry a whistle; remember six long blasts repeated at one minute intervals is the distress signal.
Do not walk alone; tell somewhere you are going.
If mist descends, return.
Observe all 'No Dogs' notices – they are generally there for very good reasons.

1

GOSFORTH AND ITS VIKING CROSS

Gosforth is a pleasing village situated near several interesting towns including Whitehaven, Egremont and Ravenglass. It is also a gateway to Wasdale. The name Gosforth is thought to mean 'ford of the geese'; these birds are depicted on a cobblestoned mosaic at the entrance to the car park. The village is surrounded by pastures and beyond stand some of the highest mountains in England. Towards the end of the walk you might like to visit, Gosforth's church of St Mary the Virgin. It is thought that a church existed in this area in the 8th century. The hogback tombs and stone cross date from before 1066. The village is not mentioned in the Domesday Book because at this date this area was part of Scotland.

Start/Finish: Gosforth car park, well signposted in the centre of village (NY067036)
Distance: 7.4km (4½ miles)
Height gain: 100m (330 ft)
Difficulty: Good paths and tracks. Some road walking

---

1. Turn left from the car park and at the Y-junction walk on along the right fork signposted 'Santon Bridge and Eskdale'. Carry on along the lane. Ignore the first footpath on the right and go on past *The Horse and Groom* to take a second footpath on the right before Rowend Bridge gateposts. The way continues on a raised causeway beside the dancing River Bleng, where dippers feed. Continue on the pleasing stiled way, with glimpses into Wasdale.

2. At the road, turn right and, after 200m take, on the left, a bridleway for Hallbolton Bridge. The track climbs gently under huge beeches, with a drop to the left into willow carr. At the attractive Hall Bolton, with

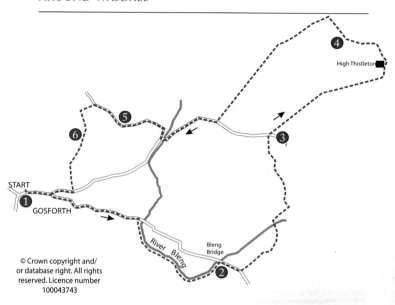

its fine buttressed barn, the track bears left to cross Hallbolton Bridge. Go with the track as it swings right and after 250m pass through a gate on the left. Climb a wide hedged way, which soon passes a copse on the left, the haunt of long tailed tits. Now to your right you can see Irton Pike, Whin Rigg and Illgill Head. Continue through a gate to walk to a second, with Bolton Head farm to your left. Carry on to the road.

3. Cross and take the track to Thistleton. The view into Wasdale Head is now magnificent. Go past Low Thistleton and, as you approach High Thistleton, the way is lined with turf and stone walls. A signposted footpath passes to the right of the farmhouse. Go through a second gate, nearest to the dwelling, and head up the pasture to a gate in the wall. Pause as you go to enjoy the views and to locate Seatallan, Buckbarrow and the tip of Middle Fell. Beyond the gate, bear steadily left to another gate in the top left corner, from where you can now look out towards the Irish Sea. Away to the right lie the misty tops of

the Ennerdale fells. Look here to notice the huge boulders used for the footings of the wall.

4. Continue steadily climbing beside the wall on your left to ascend the next two ladder-stiles and then turn left to a gate to a track. Walk left along this wide cobbled drove track to pass Between Guards farm. Follow it as it descends gently for nearly a mile to join the road to Nether Wasdale. Here turn right and walk for about 400m downhill to cross Wellington Bridge over the Bleng. Some walkers may wish to continue on the road into Gosforth, but this walk turns right beyond the racing stream and then takes a left turn. Very soon the houses are left behind and the minor road climbs steeply below lofty beeches.

5. Ignore the footpath on the left and go on to continue climbing to approach the aptly named Wind Hall. Just before the farmhouse stroll the footpath on the left. Go through a gate to walk a track and then a stile into a walled and fenced track. Climb the first of two stiles ahead, and then pass through the gate on the left between them. Descend the pasture to climb a stile halfway along a fence into Chapel Meadow. Immediately beyond is the Holy Well. Once a pilgrims' chapel stood here.

6. Continue down the pasture, bearing slightly right towards two stiles with marker posts. The footpath continues beside modern houses and then the sandstone 17th century Gosforth Hall Hotel, one of the oldest buildings in the village. Beyond the hotel is the church, where you will want to linger to see all its treasures, not forgetting the railed cork tree in the south-east corner of the churchyard. This was planted in 1833 and is thought to be the northernmost in Europe.

A thousand years ago, our Norse ancestors erected a splendid monument to express their belief that their new-found faith would ultimately prevail over paganism. The monument is the Gosforth Cross, standing 4.5m high, in the churchyard of St Mary the Virgin. The worn shaft of this, the tallest sandstone monolith in Britain, portrays a remarkable mixture of Norse legend and Christian symbolism. The lower part is rounded like a tree trunk and represents the ash tree, Yggdrasil, which the Norsemen believed supported the universe.

One of the panels of the Cross shows the crucifixion with a soldier piercing the side of Christ with a spear. Look for the evil Loki bound in chains and a deer trampling a serpent. Another huge ancient cross in the church grounds was cut down in 1789 and used as a base for a sundial.

The 'hogback' tombstones to be seen within the church are believed to have been sculpted by the same hand as carved the cross. One is the 'Warrior's Stone' and the other the 'Saint's Stone' and they are thought to have covered the graves of long forgotten chieftains.

While exploring the village look for one of the oldest buildings in Gosforth incorporated into the village hall. The latter houses the library and the Supper Room. It was built in 1628 by John and Margaret Shearwen. About 30 years later Gosforth Hall was built, using the same local sandstone and the same vernacular style by Robert Copley, a gentleman. He refused to pay the Royal Herald for his own coat of arms and instead made up one for himself.

2

IRTON WITH SANTON

The parish of Irton with Santon, in West Cumbria, is a lovely area of scattered farms, and deciduous woodland, which lies between austere fells and the sea. The River Irt hurries at first, and then idles, through pastures and hedged ways of the parish to add its waters to the River Esk. The river was once famous for its pearl-producing mussels. The church has an unusual tower and in its churchyard stands the famous 9th-century Irton Cross. This is a very pleasing walk, with magnificent views up into Ennerdale and parts of Wasdale.

Start/Finish: Bridge Inn, Santon Bridge (NY109017)
Distance: 9.5km (6 miles)
Height gain: Very little
Difficulty: A fine route through an unfrequented part of Cumbria. Easy going walk, almost level, over tracks and paths and a little road walking. Very few waymarks. After rain expect mud on some tracks

---

1. Walk uphill, left, away from car park. Go through the stile in the hedge, on the left, beyond the gate of the first house. A few steps ahead take the stile in the fence, on your right, and walk ahead across a pasture to go through a gate. Or, if the last stile into the pasture is blocked with barbed wire, walk on along the road, to take a farm gate on the left. Walk ahead until you can take the next gate, on your right, just above the topside of a small planting of conifers. You are now on the right-of-way. Pass through the next gate and then climb a stile onto a track. Cross and go through the signposted gate and walk ahead across the pasture to a gated stile opposite. Continue on to go through a gate onto a wide track.

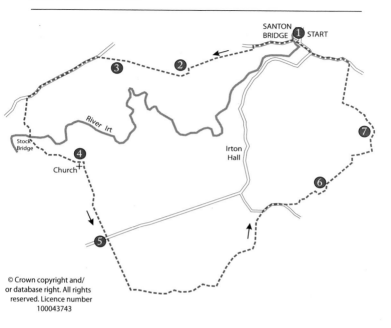

2. Turn left and then right to pass through charming Hall Santon. Wind round right, still on the track where you are soon confronted by two tracks. Ignore the obvious one, going ahead, and take the left-hand track, unsigned, that very quickly comes to a gate on your left. Beyond, continue beside a hedge on your right and a large pasture stretching away to your left. Descend steadily to step across a stream and then climb the slope to a broken stile into woodland. Here many trees have fallen and been left to lie. Climb gently, weaving round fallen trunks, with little sign of the right-of-way. Once you have reached almost level ground, begin to wind left to the side edge of wood, where there is another stile – rather hidden – out into a huge pasture.

3. Strike diagonally to the far right corner to join the road again by a gate. Turn left and walk on to pass Wardwarrow farm to your right and

a large house, Greenlands, almost hidden by trees, on your left. Just beyond the lodge to Greenlands, go through a signposted gate on the left. Aim half right over the pasture to a gate that gives access to a hedged track – the gate lies well over half way along the hedge. Turn left and descend to the picturesque stone Stock footbridge over the peacefully flowing River Irt, which you cross. Ignore the stile on the right and go on up the track. As you near the top the unusual church comes into view. Go through a gate and head over the pasture to go through another gate and then the lychgate, which stands just before the main door of the building.

There has been a church where St Paul's Church, Irton stands today since the 13th century. It is built on a hill and from it there are spectacular views of Wasdale. It was rebuilt and dedicated in 1857. The Anglian sandstone cross, seen in the churchyard, has stood for over a thousand years. It is older than the Gosforth Celtic Cross seen on Walk 1. It has obvious interlacing and knot work but some of the ornate carving has disappeared after suffering years of weathering. The cross in the corner of the churchyard is a modern copy.

4. Go inside and enjoy the peaceful church, with its banners, memorials and stained glass windows. To view the Irton Cross, with its intricate patterning, walk round to the other side of the church. The cross is believed to have marked the meeting of four ancient tracks. Then leave the churchyard by a lower gate onto a track and turn right. (Do not be tempted to continue along a fine footpath where you entered the church grounds because a small section, towards its end near Irton Hall, is often so deep in mud, it is impassable.) Follow the wide track to pass several dwellings and walk the wide way across the flat pastures to a narrow road, which you cross.

Irton Hall, a large manor house, is now converted to private homes. In its grounds stands a huge oak where Henry VI is said to have hidden in 1464 hoping for refuge during the Wars of the Roses.

5. Continue ahead along a similar track and at the next cross of tracks, turn left. Walk on to pass the access track to Wood End farm. Keep to the main track, ignoring side turns to Kitchen Ground and then later on Crag Farm. After the access track to Crag farm the track bears slightly left and carries on to join a road. Turn right and after passing a cottage and then a larch plantation, bear left along a signposted track. This delightful way eventually brings you to Parkgate farm, set among fine woodland.

6. Look for the arrow and sign on the first barn, directing you left, to pass in front of the dwelling. Beyond a gate, the pleasant track continues through the delectable woodland. In time the way curves left, climbs gently and becomes an easy-to-walk narrow path, with deer fencing to the left. On reaching a forest track, look ahead through the trees to see the attractive reed-fringed Parkgate Tarn. Then turn left and walk the good track, with a dramatic view of Irton Pike ahead, its rocky summit rearing up above its skirt of trees. The track soon curves a little left before making a right-hand curve, then, after a quarter-of-a-mile from where you joined the track, take an unsigned forest track leaving, on the left, of the main way. It can be muddy at first.

7. Climb pleasingly through the trees. Follow the way as it curves right and continues as an excellent track along the side of the forest, with low-lying West Cumbria stretching away to your left. Continue to join a road and descend left. Ignore a left turn and then a right turn, and walk on a short way to cross Santon Bridge to return to the parking area.

3

THE RIVER IRT

The delightful River Irt leaves the foot of Wast Water and meanders pleasingly through pastures and woodland. It flows under several picturesque bridges and comes close to small hamlets on its way to join the River Esk. This delightful walk starts from Santon Bridge Inn, which stands beside the river at Santon. It is the venue for the annual Biggest Liar Competition.

Start/Finish: Bridge Inn, Santon Bridge (NY109017)
Distance: 8km (5 miles)
Height gain: 130m (430ft)
Difficulty: Good paths, tracks and narrow lanes.

---

1. Cross the road and take the signposted track between the inn and the River Irt and walk on past some pretty cottages. Just before the next dwelling, look for the small footpath sign directing you to the gated footpath that continues beside the river. Stroll on to pass through pastures and beside woodland, then dawdle round a large right hand bend in the river. Keep beside the hurrying water until you can climb a stile onto a track, beside sturdy Craghouse Bridge.

2. Turn left and stride the reinforced way to reach a very narrow road, where you bear right. Continue along the hedged way and then into open pastures from where you can see two very fine bridges – one (Hollins) carries a narrow road and a few metres, right, is a slightly more humped one, which has no access. You will want to use your camera here before heading on along the glorious way, beside the Irt, to reach Hollins farm.

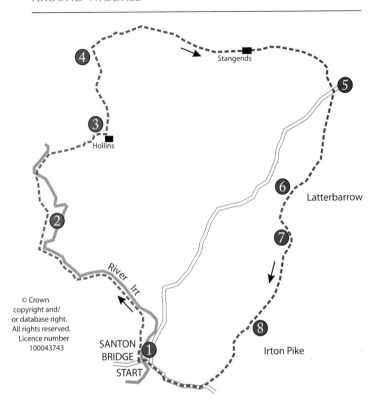

3. Pass between some outbuildings and then turn left, walking a good track, faintly waymarked on a gate. The route winds on steadily and eventually passes a small cottage and an enormous barn, tucked under a tree-clad crag. Here follow the track left, as directed by the waymarks (on the left). Walk on below the towering, sheer-sided Wrighthow Crags, almost hidden by forest trees.

4. Once past the crags, turn right immediately and walk another excellent track. This soon becomes walled on both sides, with

17

pastures running down to Irt, and scattered trees to the right. Ahead you can see the tops of the fells about Wast Water. Head on soon to pass Stangends farmhouse. Then continue through beech woodland to reach the road from Santon Bridge.

5. Cross and take the stile opposite. Cut, right, across the corner of the pasture to go through a waymarked gate. Keep on the same general direction over a large pasture, below delightful Latterbarrow, to reach the top far corner. Here take the stile into conifer woodland. Stroll on the path, covered in larch needles, and remain with it as it squeezes between the wall on your right and rhododendrons to the left.

6. At two posts of waymarks, turn right and descend to ford Merklin Beck. Beyond, wind right and walk on along a good track to reach a gate, with a stile to its left. If you climb the stile, push ahead through a larches to reach another track, where you climb left. Alternatively, go through the gate and continue along the track before turning left up the track.

7. Climb steadily and follow the way as it curves right. Ignore a tractor-wheel marked grassy track climbing right and go on along a narrowing path, which gradually descends. Ford a small stream and then continue through dark larch woodland, where fallen trees lie across the indistinct way. Wind round these, always remembering to return to the faint path, before reaching a gate. Beyond, go on through the corner of an open area, heading on a short distance to take a hand-gate into more woodland.

8. Keep beside the wall on your right, enjoying this pleasing way. After passing through the next gate, walk on to where the track divides. Here take the lower path dropping down towards the back of a semi-detached dwelling, marked on the map as London Head. Follow the rather rough path behind the houses until you can join the wide access track. Turn left and walk to the road. Turn right and descend. Ignore a left turn and go on to cross the bridge of the River Irt to return to the parking area.

Irton with Santon is a scattered parish rich in agriculture. There are many fell farms where Herdwick sheep are reared. Legend tells us that one of this breed of sheep swan ashore from a Viking ship just off Ravenglass and made its way to the hills, where pure Herdwicks graze today.

Irton with Santon is a scattered parish with the hamlets of Hall Santon, Santon and Santon Bridge nestled between the hills and the sea. It is approximately two miles long and one and a half miles wide and it is bounded by the rivers Irt and Mite. The parish is rich in agriculture with fell farms where flocks of Herdwick sheep are reared. Legend tells us that one of this breed of sheep swam ashore from a Viking ship just off Ravenglass and made its way to the hills.

Sheep in general are undemanding animals. They will nibble happily at anything in a pasture, for example, grass or rushes, and graze both to the ground. You may wonder why the sheep you pass do not get lost or need to be searched for by the farmer on his quad bike or by his dog. The reason is that Herdwicks have a strong homing instinct, which keeps them on their own land or 'heaf'. When ownership of a farm changes the sheep are not removed by the farmer but remain with the new owners and on 'their' own land.

Will Ritson lived at Wasdale Head and it is said that he was the king of liars. One year he intended to take part in the lie-telling competition at a local sports day but after listening to the tall stories told by other entrants he asked to withdraw when his turn came.' When questioned why he replied "Because I can't tell a lie". He was the winner of the competition. The Bridge Inn is an old hostelry now modernised and is the venue for many functions, including the annual Biggest Liar competition.

4

IRTON PIKE

Irton Pike is the abrupt end of a long ridge that starts from above the Wast Water Screes. On this pleasing walk to the little summit you are likely to have the fells and woodland all to yourself - other folk hurrying on to the higher tops.

Start/Finish: Lay-by on the small triangle formed by the Wasdale, Santon Bridge and Gosforth roads, east of Nether Wasdale (NY129038)
Distance: 9km (5½ miles)
Height gain: 180m (625ft)
Difficulty: A little rough fell walking.
Delightful woodland paths and tracks.
The climb up Irton Fell is quite steep so take your time and pause to enjoy the ever-increasing views.
The descent from the Pike and the return to Nether Wasdale, through glorious woodland is all easy and most attractive.
Some road walking

---

1. From the lay-by cross the road bridge over the River Irt. Take the second signposted footpath on the left, immediately beyond Flass House. Continue ahead through a pleasant area of scattered Scots pine to a gate. Beyond, stroll on to pass Flass Tarn on your right and to walk beside a wall on the left. Go through a gate and walk on, with a fine mix of beech, birch and larch to your right. At the signpost press on, uphill, until you reach a wide grassy ride. Pause here to enjoy a glimpse of Wast Water and its attendant mountains. Turn left and, still with the wall to your left, walk for 50m. At the three-armed signpost, take the right fork for Eskdale. Stride the bridleway through the mixed

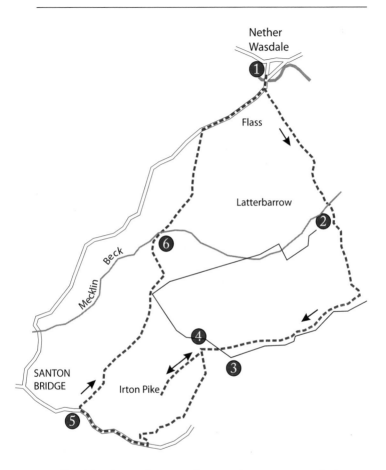

woodland, heather and pungent bog myrtle to cross two railed areas. Climb the slope to a gate in the trees and then another onto the open fell.

2. Walk ahead and then bear slightly right, across a sometimes wet

area, to join the rocky path which climbs steadily to the top of the slope. By a small cairn, 50m before the wall ahead that edges Miterdale Forest, turn right. Follow the clear green path across the fell. It keeps parallel with the forest wall but lies 100m north of it. Stride the airy fell, with its extensive views across West Cumbria, towards woodland. Enter the trees by a stile (do not take the gate and stile nearer the wall on your left), and, beyond, walk a permissive path.

3. A few metres into the trees a forest ride goes away left. Ignore this but note it for your return. Go ahead through the conifers. Suddenly and dramatically, through the trees at the edge of the woodland, you can see the lovely mound of the Pike. Follow the clear path to the summit and stay awhile, lazing on a cushion of heather, to take in the wonderful view. Look towards Wast Water to see Red Pike, Yewbarrow and Kirk Fell to the left of Great Gable. Nearer are Whin Rigg and Illgill Head, both overshadowing the lake.

4. Return from the top to the ride that you noted when you entered the forest, now on your right. Bear right and continue downhill to join a wider track. Go on downhill. Watch out for a narrow path that continues to drop down, going off right again. This brings you steadily downhill to join a wide track. Turn left and walk to a stile beside a double gate to the road to Santon Bridge. Turn right and follow it as it descends. Where the road makes a sharp swing left, take the signposted long access track on the right. Just before the gate to dwellings named London Head, take the footpath on the right, to go behind the cottages.

5. Carry on to join a forest ride and continue on (left). Pass through two gates and continue as directed by the footpath sign through an open area. Enter a dark plantation where the path underfoot, though not waymarked, is clear, leading you to another open area. Follow the path through the delightful clearing beneath the flaring Shepherd Crags. Then follow the path downhill. A few metres before Mecklin Beck, turn right to walk another track which brings you to a ford over the beck, which you cross on convenient boulders.

6. After a few steps ahead, take a waymarked narrow footpath leading left. Follow it as it swings right and continues along the edge of a plantation under the magnificent slopes of Latterbarrow. Watch out for the stile on the left, where two walls come together. Beyond the stile, stroll diagonally across the large pasture to a gate in the bottom far corner. Continue on in the same direction to a ladder-stile to the road. Turn right to walk to cross the bridge over the Irt and to regain the start of the walk.

> *As you walk the road below Irton Fell look on the right for the stone memorial in memory of William Malkinson, a Wesleyan local preacher, who died at this spot on Sunday, February 21 1886. The large inscription ends: 'BE YE ALSO READY'.*

From the summit of Irton Pike there is a path dropping downhill to the Santon Bridge road, but it is very steep and frequently muddy and slippery. This is best ignored. Part of this walk uses a path taken, in the opposite direction, in Walk 3.

Flass Tarn, surrounded by grass, lies among scattered pines. It is a charming corner passed early on in this walk. But in a drought (rare in the Wasdale) it dries up and perhaps does not merit being called a tarn. Its banks support kingcups and it is frequently visited by herons.

5

MITERDALE

This pleasing walk takes you through Miterdale, the lovely, lonely valley between Eskdale and Wasdale. It then continues high onto Eskdale Moor, above the dale, to view the stone circles and numerous small hut circles. These suggest that during the mild, drier weather of the early and middle Bronze Age people moved up to occupy the higher fells. When the climate changed, the occupants of these settlements moved down into the valleys. On a sunny day these high pastures are idyllic but after a series of wet summers you can quite understand such a migration.

Start/Finish: From the free parking on a wide open area by the River Mite (NY146012) at the end of a narrow road.
This is reached from Eskdale Green, signposted for the school, and passes through quiet countryside for about 1.5km (1 mile).
Distance: 8.8km (5½ miles)
Height gain: 250m (825ft)
Difficulty: Reasonably good tracks and paths, but they can be boggy in parts

---

1. From the parking area, cross the bridge over the River Mite and follow the reinforced track as it heads into the dale, with Scafell in the far distance. Go past Low Place farm, with it famous sign on the left-hand wall beyond. Ignore the ford and keep left of the river, continuing over pastures to pass through two gates with stiles. Walk ahead along a rough path close to a conifer plantation on your left. Pass through a gate gap and drop half right on a path towards the river. Go on ahead in front of the Bakerstead Outdoor Centre for Egremont School and then cross a pasture to pass through a gap in the boundary wall, shadowed by a large ash.

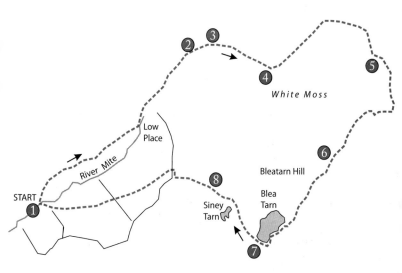

2. Turn right to pass through the 'spooky' ruins of Miterdale Head farm.

> *The legend associated with Miterdale Head farm tells of*
> *a happening while the farmer was away at Whitehaven*
> *market. His wife gave shelter to an old woman who*
> *arrived at the farm door in the dusk after crossing the*
> *moor. When the old woman fell asleep by the fire, her*
> *mouth dropped open wide and her wig slipped revealing*
> *that she was an ugly man. 'She' was clutching a knife. The*
> *wife fearing that he was a robber and that she and her*
> *baby might be attacked, fetched a ladle of boiling tallow*
> *fat (for candles) and poured it down the open throat of*
> *the sleeping fellow. Alas he choked to death. When the*
> *farmer returned next day, he was met by his demented*
> *wife, and a corpse. He buried the body and eventually*

*they moved away from this lonely corner and only then
did he tell this story.*

3. Beyond, descend right towards a small arched bridge, which you should view from the side, where its superb workmanship can be appreciated. Stroll on a few steps to join a path that runs along the other side of the river, and turn left. Pass through a gate and turn right as directed by an arrow on a slate sign. Ascend the almost pathless way beside a plantation on the right. At the top corner of the forest, go through a gate on the right and then pass through a gate gap in a wall. Turn left and begin your walk over high-level moorland.

4. Follow the narrow path, keeping parallel with the wall on your left. At the first division take the right branch. After rain this section of the path can be squelchy but not seriously so. Where the path veers steadily away from the wall and gains height it becomes dry and pleasant to walk. It divides several times and you should take the most heavily used. After passing a large boulder beside the path you arrive at the first of the granite circles and close by is another where you will want to pause and then, head on to reach a very large circle with hut circles within.

5. Climb left on a short path to a hillock from where there is a spectacular view into Eskdale and of all the dramatic fells around. Then descend a few steps on the path to a cross of paths. Turn right to follow a narrow path leading to a very obvious track continuing over the moorland slopes. Carry on until you reach a distinct Y-junction of paths where you take the higher grassy right branch. This takes you round the base of a hill, and then winds on right to edge a large flat area, which might once have been the bed of a small tarn.

6. At a large pointed cairn continue on through the cairned hillocks, still winding a little right, to come to the brow of a hillock marked with another large cairn. Here you might wish to descend the grassy trod that takes you down through a splendid gully to the side of Blea Tarn. Or you may prefer to take the very short, right hand path to the top of

Bleatarn Hill, from where there is a superb view down to the mountain tarn. A few steps back from the edge, a little path takes you down the slope to join the path in the gully. Then turn right and descend more to walk along the shore of the quiet pool, where you might see tufted ducks.

> Blea Tarn is enclosed on three sides by low heather-covered outcrops. The outlet beck leaves to the south-west where the land opens out. Before piped water arrived in the valley, Eskdale, below, it supplied water to the farms of the valley.

7. Wind round right on the path at the foot of the tarn, keeping the tarn to your right. Remain on this path as it curves left round another large rocky hillock. Follow this as it winds right, with reedy Sineytarn Moss to you left. On joining a wider path, turn left and continue on beside the Moss, part of which is clear of reeds to justify the name tarn – but only just.

8. Follow the distinct path as it leaves the tarn behind and soon the tops of the Miterdale plantations come into view. Watch out for a faint division of the path and take the right branch. This descends a little and then it winds left along the foot of a hillock, on your left, and brings you to the corner of the plantation high above Low Place farm. Turn right and descend a short path beside walled conifers now to your left, to arrive at a gate into the forest. Turn left, go through the gate, and follow the wide track through the trees, a great contrast with the open slopes above, and descend for just over half a mile to where you have parked.

6

WAST WATER

Wast Water was voted people's most favourite view in Great Britain, in a television series. This walk gives you a chance to see if you agree. After passing through pastures, woodland, and along the side of the River Irt, the way continues beside the lovely lake. The route continues over fine pastures to Buckbarrow farm, before returning through meadows and rough pastures to view all the charming attractions of Nether Wasdale.

Start/Finish: Nether Wasdale triangle of roads, on the north side of the Cinderdale Bridge over the River Irt (NY129038).
Distance: 10.5km (6½ miles)
Height gain: Virtually level walking
Difficulty: Good paths and tracks. Many gates and signposts have been renewed and are a pleasure to use.

Nether Wasdale, often known as Strands, is set in a quiet hollow with superb views of the mountains. In 1897 a maypole was erected on the village green to commemorate the sixty years reign of Queen Victoria. It still has a charming maypole in use today.

1. Re-cross the bridge and pass The Flass, a sturdy white house on the left, and, beyond, take the footpath, left, signposted for Eskdale. Walk ahead over a pasture, keeping parallel with the wall on your left. Climb the stile over a fence, a short way along from the wall, to view a delightful small tarn. Keep to the left of the latter, still remaining beside the wall on your left. Go through the gate in the top left corner and walk on with fine deciduous woodland to the right. At the T-junction of tracks, bear left, still keeping beside the wall on the left. At the next

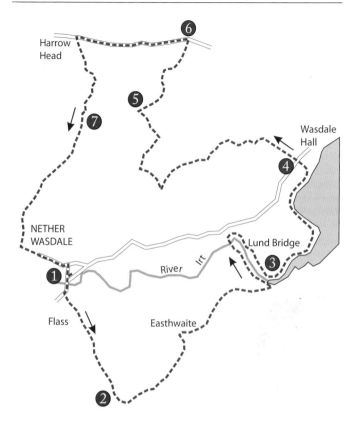

footpath, signposted Wasdale, bear left again with the wall. The path is pleasing to walk as it carries on with a conifer plantation to your right. Where the trees cease, go through a gate and stroll on along a glorious green trod, with a grand view of the Wasdale mountains ahead.

2. Follow the track as it winds a little left to pass through a gate. Stroll the track as it curves right to pass in front of Easthwaite farm. Remain on

the good reinforced track, passing through metal gates and continue where it winds right as directed by an arrow. The distinct way then descends gently towards the outflow from Wast Water. Here take the kissing gate on the left, directing you into the delectable woodland beside the River Irt, on your right. Carry on beside the hurrying water to reach Lund Bridge, which you cross. Go through a kissing gate, on the right, into more woodland and turn sharp right to walk along the opposite bank of the Irt. This is a permissive path through Low Wood. It keeps close the river and then the lakeshore itself. Here you might spot bullfinches and nuthatches.

3. Soon you can see more of the mountains at the head of the lake, and The Screes (550m high) to your right. When a path comes in on your left, join this and walk right. This wanders about a bit but soon returns to the side of the lake. Eventually you reach several seats. Ignore the first and sit on either the second or third from where there are superb views over Wast Water. Remain beside the lake as you pass through a gate onto an open grassy area below a fine house, used by the Youth Hostel Association. Go through a second gate and carry on through rhododendrons to climb a ladder-stile. Turn left to walk a few steps to the road.

4. Turn left, cross the cattle grid and walk on to take, on the right, a signposted track that runs beside a high walled enclosure on your right. At the wall end, head on along a lumpy path to climb a fine ladder-stile. Beyond, walk half left on a grassy trod through rushes. The way gets a little lost and then re-emerges and winds right to a small signpost. Turn left and walk a distinct track. Ignore a signposted path on the left to Woodhow and the road, and continue on to a clearly signposted stile and gate ahead.

5. Climb the stile and turn right to walk in the direction of Buckbarrow. Stroll the delightful green track, with a fence to the right and lined with oaks on the left. Go through a gate and walk on through birch, and at the boundary wall go, right, along a bridleway, clearly arrowed on a piece of slate. Ignore a gate on the left and remain on the bridleway,

with a wall to the left, as it curves gently left. Then go over a stile beside the gate across the track. Go on ahead along the grassy way to cross a tractor bridge and dawdle on with a glorious flower-lined stream to your left. Pass through the next gate and head towards the crags of Buckbarrow. Beyond the next gate wind right with the track to walk on towards the farm along a splendid grassy walled way. Keep to left of the farm and then walk a short track to join the road.

6. Walk left for half a mile along the generally quiet way. Just after crossing a stream, turn left into a wide access track to pass a cottage, on the right, and then a farm on the left. Walk on down the track to cross a ford by a little plank bridge and continue to a signed junction of tracks. Here go straight ahead beside the wall on your right. The grassy trod leads to a waymarked gate and then on to pass through a second gate (unmarked), now with the wall to your left. Where the latter turns away left, go on ahead to walk a stretch of duckboarding and then climb the stile over the wall into rough pasture.

7. A narrow but distinct path leads on through dense gorse and bracken. Follow the path as it climbs a little and then descends easily out of the tangle of vegetation to come to a stile and a difficult gate. Once over the stile, walk on with oak woodland to your right. Carry on ahead, keeping left of a pristine caravan and campsite. Wind round left with the wide track, soon to arrive at Nether Wasdale. To return to the triangle of roads you turn left and walk on a short way to take a right turn. But it would be a shame to miss the attractive village – so turn right, and visit the lovely little church on the right. Walk on across the green sward with the maypole. Carry on a short way, perhaps to enjoy some refreshments at one of the two inns, The Screes and the Strands Hotel, one on each side of the road. Just beyond The Screes stands a very interesting drinking fountain. As you return to the parking area, peep inside the charming war memorial, on the right, just before you turn right to where you have parked.

Nether Wasdale, on the River Irt, is sometimes known as
Strands. As it has a church some would call it a village, but

31

with so few dwellings it is really just a hamlet. The little white church is dedicated to St Michael and All Angels and is built like a barn, the nave and chancel are one. Go inside to enjoy the ornate ceiling with texts and cherubs looking down from above. Some of the fine carvings came from York Minster and the alms-box stands on a cherub's head.

The youth hostel, passed below on this walk, is housed in the lovely Wasdale Hall. It is reputed to be haunted by the wife of a previous owner who lived there in the early 19th century and whose small child was drowned in the lake. A ghostly figure has been seen walking along the edge of the lake.

At point 6 you walk the quiet road below Buckbarrow Fell, which faces the Screes across Wast Water. The fell stands, stony and steep with ledges of grass and heather, at the end of a long grassy ridge, part of Seatallan, which you view from the next walk in this book. A small stream from Buckbarrow feeds into Tosh Tarn, all that remains of the ice-age lake that once covered Nether Wasdale. Just below the farm mentioned in point 6, look over the wall on the right to spot the little tarn.

7

GREENDALE TARN
AND MIDDLE FELL

The lonely, secret Greendale Tarn lies in a short U-shaped valley, high in the fells, between Seatallan and Middle Fell. As you approach Wast Water, Buckbarrow and Middle Fell are the shapely guardians to your left. They are subsidiary slopes of Seatallan, the bulky fell hidden from the main valley. This is a challenging walk but be prepared to turn back if the weather changes or the route becomes too difficult.

Start/Finish: Verge at Greendale (NY145056).
If approaching from the south end of Wast Water, take the
first left turn and drive on for half a mile to park on the right.
Distance: 5.5m (3½ miles).
Height gain: 500m (1650ft)
Difficulty: A steepish climb to the ravine and then a rocky climb
onto grassy flats about the tarn.
The ascent and descent of Middle Fell is rocky,
but it is not as difficult as it looks as there is always a little
path to follow. <u>Do NOT attempt in the mist.</u>
Expect a wet walk near the tarn after rain.

---

1. From the parking area follow the signposted footpath north, with the craggy slopes of Buckbarrow, and Greendale Gill, to your left. Climb the zigzagging path, which ascends quite steeply. At the top of the slope the path divides, the branch to the right being your return route. The left branch, now less steep, continues though Greendale Gill, high above the mountain beck, which steadily descends in white-topped falls and cascades. On the opposite side of the gill narrow

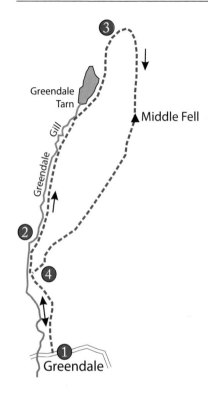

becks hurtle down several gills and these are aptly named Tongues Gills.

2. Follow the now rougher path through the gill and, where it becomes less steep, the cliffs of Middle Fell come into view. Carry on up the sometimes wet way until you reach Greendale Tarn, concealed until the last moment by a ridge of moraine. After a pause here, continue along the right (east) side of the tarn until you reach its end, keeping above soggy ground.

3. Bear slightly right to pick up a narrow path that has come down from Seatallan. Turn right on this and follow it steadily up through the many rocky outcrops towards the highest part of Middle Fell. As you go, look down on the tarn, held in its hanging valley by glacial drift. Middle Fell's summit cairn, 582m, lies to the left of the path, at the edge of a steep drop, and at this high point the real reward of the walk awaits. You can see all of Wast Water and also Seatallan, Haycock, Scoat Fell, Red Pike, Kirk Fell, Yewbarrow, Great Gable and the Scafells. Rejoin the path to begin your descent of this delightful little rugged fell. Where the path leads to the edge of rocky outcrops, which involve some scrambling, you can enjoy the climb down or find an easier grassy way by moving to the right or the left.

From the cairn on Middle Fell, 582m (1908ft) high, you have a splendid view of Wast Water. On the way up Greendale Gill look for attractive Tongues Gills and their waterfalls on the opposite side of the beck.

Between Seatallan, not visited on this walk, and Middle Fell, is a short U-shaped valley, carved by a glacier as it flowed from the high fells. Held in this is Greendale Tarn, 290m long and 106m wide and it follows the shape of the valley. Its maximum depth is 9m. The southern end of the valley was cut off by the great glacier that flowed down Wasdale and this resulted in the Greendale Beck falling steeply to Wasdale.

4. After just over a mile from the tarn, you join the path taken on your outward route. From here you have a dramatic view of The Screes, the sheer slopes of Illgill Head, which descend into the water to a depth of 88m. Drop downhill to return to the parking area.

In his "Tours to the British Mountains", Thomas Wilkinson, well-known for his poem 'The Solitary Reaper', says in his piece 'Wastwater 2':

"The Lake is wholly hidden 'till your Feet touch it,' as one may say, and to a Stranger the Burst would be almost overwhelming. The Lake itself seen from the Foot appears indeed of too regular shape; exactly like the sheet of Paper on which I am writing, except it is still narrower in respect to its length. In reality however the Lake widens as it ascends and at the head is very considerably broader than at the foot."

This description of Thomas' first sighting of Wast Water has not changed over the years and it is just beyond this great 'burst' of delight that you turn left to park for Middle Fell.

8

Over Beck
and the skirts of Yewbarrow

The view from the foot of Wast Water was recently voted as the best in the country. It is a wonderful amphitheatre of fells with Great Gable directly ahead. To Gable's right, peep the Scafells over Lingmell. To the left lies 'little' Yewbarrow, stealing the scene with its splendid southern prow coming down steeply to the shore of the lake. This walk takes you up beside Over Beck, a lovely mountain torrent full of waterfalls. It returns below Yewbarrow with a superb view of the Wast Water Screes ahead.

Start/Finish: Overbeck Bridge car park by Wast Water (NY168068), just beyond Overbeck Bridge, on the left, overlooking the lake.
Distance: 9km (5½ miles)
Height gain: 250m/825ft
Difficulty: Challenging in parts. If you find Gosforth Crag Moss too wet to cross, you will have to turn round and retrace your outward route but at the same time you will enjoy the dramatic views down into Wasdale.

---

1. Follow the path out of the car path and walk close beside Over Beck. Follow the narrow path as it climbs the side of the gorge to join the main track above. Pass through a kissing gate, ignore a path climbing right towards Yewbarrow and continue ahead. Very soon the land to the left of the path drops steeply to the beck and deciduous trees clothe the ravine but not so close as to hide the innumerable cascades. The path climbs steadily and the sides of the beck become flatter and the fellside more open. Continue on the delightful way until you reach a footbridge over a narrow canyon, which you cross.

2. Pass through a gap in a wall, turn right and go through another gap in the wall ahead. Then strike uphill to find a wide grassy path and continue on to cross Brimfell Beck on convenient boulders. (The beck lives up to its name and if it is in spate it is sensible to return to re-cross bridge and turn left up the less well trodden path on the other side of the beck.) Carry on along the path until it fades and then walk on, over short grass, across Great Gosforth Moss, remaining parallel with Over Beck now a tiny stream. Keep well right of Great Knott and walk the often boggy way.

3. Just before the scree slopes of Dore Head, look for the path coming in on your right, and turn onto this for your return. The track contours around the fellside, high above Over Beck, but passing well below Long Crag and Dropping Crag, on Yewbarrow's skirts, for just over a mile. As you go, look for the jagged tops of The Screes on the far side of Wast Water. Seemingly, almost at one's feet, lie the bright green

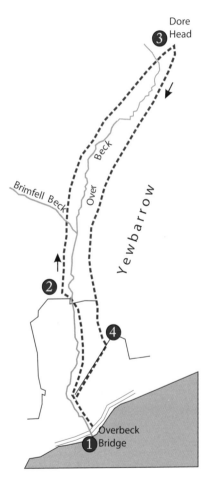

37

fields of Bowderdale, wrested with such effort from the sometimes unsympathetic hand of nature, and now enclosed by neat stone walls.

4. Eventually you reach a ladder-stile. Beyond descend, right, the steepish track, with the wall to your right, to reach the kissing gate taken at the outset of your walk. Beyond, follow the track down to the car park.

> The car park just beyond Overbeck Bridge, on the shores, of Wast Water is almost hidden from the road by oak, rowan and whitebeam. The beck races alongside and the air is filled with the sound of falling water, a sound that is to accompany the walker throughout a day spent in the valley of Overbeck.

> The footpath keeps close beside the mountain stream. Ahead graceful larches lean over the first of the many falls on this turbulent beck's headlong race to the lake. On the opposite bank cushions of heather luxuriate in the spray. Chaffinches and wrens flit through the branches of birch and rowan that line the small gorge, their songs unheard, drowned by the noise of hurrying water. In summer tormentil brightens the pasture on either side of the path and towards autumn harebells line the way. Where the path descends towards the beck ash, oak, rowan and holly clothe the ravine and here you might spot jays feasting on dropped acorns. About the slopes flit meadow pipits and from the tops of boulders, wheatears chack, chack plaintively or sing their pleasing small songs.

> Among these high fells are three tarns: Scoat Tarn is the source of Nether Beck, Low Tarn is the source of Brimfell Beck and Over Beck, and Greendale Tarn feeds into Greendale Gill, see Walk 7.

9

BURNMOOR TARN
AND THE COFFIN ROUTE

This is an exhilarating walk that takes you from Wasdale Head to Burnmoor Tarn using the old coffin route. The paths can be boggy in parts and quite exposed, but to compensate for this are fine views and a glorious feeling of being among the fells and away from the hustle and bustle of modern life. Families will love the legends associated with the coffin route and youngsters should watch out for a ghostly horse.

Start/Finish: Car park by camp site at Brackenclose.
Access is gained by a track off the valley road, on the right,
just after the head of Wast Water (NY182075)
Distance: 8km (5 miles)
Height gain: 306m (1,000 ft)
Difficulty: Reasonable paths for most of the way but after
rain this can be a rather wet walk – but a lovely one

---

1. Follow the track, left, to cross Lingmell Bridge. Then bear left along the signed bridleway for Eskdale, keeping beside the beck for a short distance. Turn right before the Fell and Rock Club hut, with the wall to your right, to pass through a gate. Go on along the path and through the next gate. Ascend a steepish stony way. Beyond the next gate, go over a bridge and step over several streams, which after rain hurry down the slopes. Continue beside woodland to your right.

2. Go with the path as it leaves the wall and carries on up over the well cairned open fell. Water settles here after rain and to cross almost dry foot, keep beside the cairns. As you go, ignore trods on your right. To

your left you might spot a
pile of stones, larger than
a cairn and a faint path
leading to it. This is known
as Maiden Castle. Shortly
after this large Burnmoor
Tarn comes into view.

*The way to the tarn is
known as the Coffin
Route. As there was
no consecrated
ground for burials
at Wasdale, the
dead of the valley
had to be carried
on horseback to
the graveyard at
St Katharine's in
Eskdale. One day,
in a gale, the hat
of the mourner
leading the horse
carrying the body
of a young man,
blew off frightening
the horse and
causing it to bolt.
The mourners
searched all day for
the horse and its
burden without out
success and with
the onset of snow
had to return to the
valley. The man's*

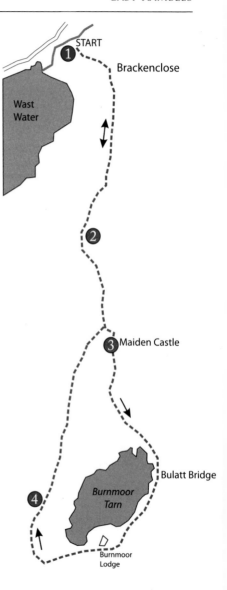

mother was very upset by the unburied body of her son. A few months later she died. As she was being carried to Eskdale, the horse bolted and carried his burden away into the mist. The mourners searched as they had done earlier and strangely found the first horse, thin and weak still carrying the man's body. They carried on to bury him. The mother's body, and the horse carrying her, were never found.

3. Press on, climbing gently, to pass a small walled pasture on your right and to reach the brow of the slope. Beyond, follow the cairned path, descending steadily to Bulatt Bridge. From here the track begins to climb again on its way to Eskdale but this walk, in a few steps, leaves the bridleway, right, and winds round the tarn, in the direction of Burnmoor Lodge, once a shooting bothy. Keep to the path above the building and go on along the path to the southern tip of the tarn. Continue on, uphill for a few steps, to reach a cairn. Turn right and follow the path, with a fine view of the tarn, now on your right, and its cradling fells.

Burnmoor Tarn is the third largest in Lakeland, the deepest part is about 14m (44ft). Its edge is unbroken by any promontories and it lies in high moorland hidden away from the valleys below. This is where early Britons built their homes. To the north of the tarn lies Maiden Castle, which could have been used for defence by these ancient folk. On Brats Moss, a mile south-west of the tarn, are stone circles with hut circles inside of them and nearby a standing stone (see Walk 5).

4. Stroll on, keeping above the walled enclosure passed on your outward route. Eventually you join your outward track, along which you retrace your outward route. If you miss this and reach a wall, turn right and follow it until you do attain the track to return to Brackenclose.

10

MOSEDALE
AND RITSON'S FORCE

Two hundred years ago, William Wordsworth said, when looking down
from Great Gable at the head of Wasdale:
"Half a dozen neat dwellings scattered upon a plain of meadow and
corn ground, intersected with stone walls apparently innumerable, like
a piece of lawless patchwork, or an array of mathematical figures, such
as in the ancient schools of geometry might have been sportively and
fantastically traced out upon sand." This walk explores some of this plain
meadow and lawless patchwork walls.

Start/Finish: Car park, by the campsite at Brackenclose (NY182075).
Distance: 9.5km (6 miles)
Height gain: 150m (500ft)
Difficulty: Delightful on a summer's day during a dry spell and
on a bright crisp day when the ground of Mosedale is frozen.
Expect some athletic bog hopping after rain.

1. Turn ~~left~~ from the car park and walk on to cross the wide bridge
over the beck that races down Lingmell Gill. Continue ahead beside
the hurrying water to pass to the left of the Fell and Rock Club hut. Go
on to take the footbridge over the beck and through the gate beyond.
Here, leave the path beside Lingmell Gill and walk a narrow path,
which climbs steadily uphill.

2. Where the path joins a wider one, turn left and pause. Below lies
Wasdale Head, guarded by Yewbarrow, Kirkfell and Great Gable, with
Pillar standing austere and aloof beyond Mosedale. Enjoy a bird's-eye

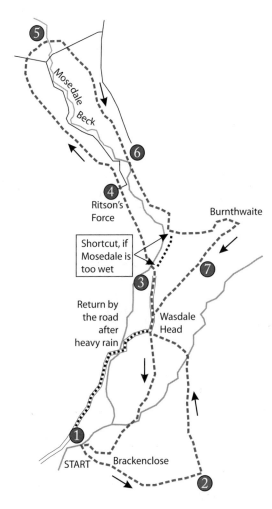

Mosedale Beck

5

6

4
Ritson's
Force

Shortcut, if
Mosedale is
too wet

3

Return by
the road
after
heavy rain

Wasdale
Head

Burnthwaite

7

1

START

Brackenclose

2

view of the sturdy walls. Go on gently downhill, beneath the steep slopes of Lingmell. Cross the footbridge over Lingmell Beck and walk ahead, following a line of posts to a gate and a stile, to the right, onto the fell road. Turn right and walk towards Wasdale Head Inn.

The Wasdale Head Inn was once the home of Will Ritson. He was a farmer, a huntsman, a wrestler and a keen drinker. In the 1850s he added a wing to his farmhouse and got a drinks licence. But he is remembered more for his title as 'the biggest liar in England'.

43

3. Follow the signpost which lies beyond the inn and before the shop and cottages. Stride left and then right upstream to cross the glorious slate packhorse bridge over Mosedale Beck. Bear right across the pasture beyond, to a gate signed Ritson's Force. Follow the track, with the wall to your right, towards woodland and take a wall gap beside the wood, on the right, and walk forward through an idyllic copse. The thundering of the falling water will lead you to the lovely waterfalls.

4. Return to the path into Mosedale by passing through a wall gap, turn right and continue to a kissing gate, with a dramatic view of Pillar ahead. Beyond, the path continues over higher ground to avoid a large wet area by the wall. Look up left to see the sharp end of Yewbarrow, Stirrup Crag and Dore Head screes. Continue on the clear way, keeping well above a sheepfold, aiming for a ladder-stile over the next wall. From the top of this, look ahead to see a huge rock known as the Y-boulder – and labelled in this way on some maps – because of the shape of a crack it bears. An arrow at the foot of the boulder directs you right, across the valley floor. Walkers may be able to cross Mosedale Beck here by hopping across boulders, but if the river is in spate you will have to wade, with care, or sadly retrace your steps.

5. Beyond the beck, turn right and bear diagonally left, following a narrow sheep trod, and stepping across several small streams. Aim for a gate and a large modern sheep pen beyond the wall, slightly uphill, 250m from the main beck. Leave the pen by a stile to join, and walk right, the Black Sail Pass track, which comes over from Ennerdale and is the climbers' path to Pillar. Beyond the next stile a good track continues beside a wall. Ahead is a spectacular view of Scafell. Follow the track as it curves right to pass through the next gate. (This is the point where you rejoin the walk, having re-crossed the packhorse bridge and turned left if you have had to retrace your steps because Mosedale and its beck were too difficult to cross.)

6. Beyond the gate, turn left to walk a glorious way between walls, accompanied by Fog Mire Beck, which you cross several times by sturdy footbridges, to reach Burnthwaite farm to join a stony track.

Follow the track, right, between the outbuildings, to join another track, where you turn right. Look for the enormously thick walls, and for the clearance cairns in the stone-free pastures. Go on to the tiny church of St Olaf, set in its ring of large yews.

> *The church of St Olaf measures 13m by 6m and is one of England's smallest. It has three windows, one of them a memorial to Queen Victoria. Look at the gravestones in the tiny churchyard, which gives the church its name of being the climbers' church.*

7. Stroll on to cross the triangle of grass, used for parking, to join the narrow road walked earlier. Beyond a signposted gate, on the left, take the track to the right. Go over a small footbridge and continue to cross the next two streams by convenient stones. Once over the next stile, follow a clear track through a vast area of gorse to take another gate. Bear right along the river bank – often just a river of boulders. Cross the riverbed, picking the best way and once on the opposite bank turn right and walk on to go though a gate. Stroll on to take a gate on the left and continue on the track that leads to Brackenclose. Turn right to rejoin your car. If there has been a lot of rain you may prefer to continue on the valley road and then turn left to the car park.

> *The fine stone walls that network the dale were built between the middle of the 18th and 19th century to enclose moorland, previously common land, to provide pasture and shelter for sheep. The stone used was either taken from the open moor or from the beck bottom. Any excess stone was gathered into huge mounds known as clearance cairns. Pause as you cross the fine bridge behind the inn. Packhorse bridges were constructed without sides allowing the horses to carry heavy, wide loads in their panniers, which could project on either side over the river.*